$\mathcal{L}$augh and the world laughs with you.
Cry and you cry with your girlfriends.

— *Laurie Kuslansky*

Blue Mountain Arts®
Bestselling Books

By Susan Polis Schutz:
To My Daughter, with Love, on the Important Things in Life
To My Son, with Love
I Love You

Is It Time to Make a Change?
by Deanna Beisser

To the Love of My Life
by Donna Fargo

100 Things to Always Remember... and One Thing to Never Forget
For You, Just Because You're Very Special to Me
To the One Person I Consider to Be My Soul Mate
by Douglas Pagels

Being a Teen ...Words of Advice from Someone Who's Been There
The Girl's Guide to Loving Yourself
by Diane Mastromarino

girls rule ...a very special book created especially for girls
by Ashley Rice

A Lifetime of Love ...Poems on the Passages of Life
by Leonard Nimoy

Anthologies:
42 Gifts I'd Like to Give to You
Always Believe in Yourself and Your Dreams
The Bond Between a Mother and Son Lasts Forever
A Daughter Is Forever
For You, My Daughter
Friends for Life
I Love You, Mom
I'm Glad You Are My Sister
The Joys and Challenges of Motherhood
The Language of Recovery ...and Living Life One Day at a Time
Life Can Be Hard Sometimes ...but It's Going to Be Okay
Marriage Is a Promise of Love
May You Always Have an Angel by Your Side
Take Each Day One Step at a Time
Teaching and Learning Are Lifelong Journeys
There Is Greatness Within You, My Son
These Are the Gifts I'd Like to Give to You
Think Positive Thoughts Every Day
Thoughts to Share with a Wonderful Teenager
To My Child
With God by Your Side ...You Never Have to Be Alone

Girlfriends Are the BEST Friends of All

A Tribute to Laughter, Secrets, Girl Talk, Chocolate, Shopping... and Everything Else Women Share

Edited by Suzanne Moore

Blue Mountain Press™

Boulder, Colorado

Library of Congress Control Number: 2004092878
ISBN: 0-88396-844-4

ACKNOWLEDGMENTS appear on page 64.

Certain trademarks are used under license.
BLUE MOUNTAIN PRESS is registered in U.S. Patent and Trademark Office.

Manufactured in the United States of America.
First Printing: 2004

 This book is printed on recycled paper.

This book is printed on fine quality, laid embossed, 80 lb. paper. This paper has been specially produced to be acid free (neutral pH) and contains no groundwood or unbleached pulp. It conforms with all the requirements of the American National Standards Institute, Inc., so as to ensure that this book will last and be enjoyed by future generations.

Blue Mountain Arts, Inc.

P.O. Box 4549, Boulder, Colorado 80306

Contents

Girlfriends Are the BEST Friends of All

Where would I be if it weren't for my women friends? We laugh together, cry together, compare notes on our children, and complain about our jobs. We do lunch, we go shopping, we borrow each other's clothes, and we talk on the phone... for hours sometimes. I depend on them for so much — company, comfort, guidance, advice, and sometimes a good swift kick when I need it!... Give me the support of a few good women friends, and I can do almost anything!

— BJ Gallagher

Girlfriends are such an important part of life,
and whether we see them all the time or not,
they are crucial in the way we see
and interact with the world.
Girlfriends stand by us and are there
to help through challenges,
illnesses, heartaches, and
all sorts of worries and decisions.
Girlfriends keep us from losing our minds,
our faith, and sometimes
our spouses or our keys.
Girlfriends play different roles, but
each one is important.
Some are the shoppers,
others the phone talkers,
some know just what to say
when there's a tragedy,
and others make us laugh.
The one thing they all have in common
is that they bring camaraderie,
contentment, security, and joy
into our lives.

— Barbara Cage

A Woman Needs a Friend...

*T*o let us bare our souls.
To allow us to free the emotions,
secrets, fantasies, and dreams
that are sometimes beyond the
comprehension of
other people in our lives.
To release our frustrations to,
and whose frustrations
we can help relieve.
To laugh, cry, rejoice,
and share with.
To just be there.

As women, we are not
always strong,
but together we can make it.
True friendship is an
important piece of being a woman.
It helps to know that we have
a place to go where there is
a smile and an ear when needed.
It helps to know we have
friends.

— Susan M. Catalano

Any woman who sews
or knits, or weaves,
blends colors in a tapestry
or creates a patchwork quilt,
knows by the feel
that a single thread is weak
but the weaving,
the blending,
the intertwining
with many others
makes it strong.

Any woman alone,
without friends
to sustain her,
to nurture and support,
to hold with loving arms,
like a single thread, is weak.
But the weaving,
the loving,
the nurturing of others,
the networks of friendship
make her strong.

— Anonymous

I imagine we are all jigsaw puzzles with little parts of us missing: small flaws, things we don't do very well (organize, cook, remember birthdays); or places where we hurt or need comfort or an infusion of another's joy. Then a certain friend comes along and fits into that little open place, making our life more complete, and suddenly we realize how much we'd been missing that connection, that little puzzle piece.

— Becky Freeman

Get Yourself Some Girlfriends!

$\mathcal{I}$ sat under a pecan tree in the hot Texas sun on a summer day, drinking iced tea and getting to know my new sister-in-law, Estelle. Not much older than I, but already the mother of three, Estelle seemed to me experienced and wise.

"Get yourself some girlfriends," she advised, clinking the ice cubes in her glass. "You are going to need girlfriends. Go places with them; do things with them."

What a funny piece of advice, I thought. Hadn't I just gotten married? Hadn't I just joined the couple-world? I was a married woman, for goodness sake, not a young girl who needed girlfriends. But I listened to this new sister-in-law. I got myself some girlfriends.

As the years tumbled by, one after another, I gradually came to understand that Estelle knew what she was talking about. Here is what I know about girlfriends:

Girlfriends bring casseroles and scrub your bathroom when you are sick.
Girlfriends keep your children and keep your secrets.
Girlfriends give advice when you ask for it.
Sometimes you take it, sometimes you don't.

Girlfriends don't always tell you that you're right,
  but they're usually honest.
Girlfriends still love you, even when they don't
  agree with your choices.
Girlfriends might send you a birthday card,
  but they might not. It does not matter in
  the least.
Girlfriends laugh with you, and you don't need
  canned jokes to start the laughter.
Girlfriends pull you out of jams.
Girlfriends don't keep a calendar that lets them
  know who hosted the other last.
Girlfriends are there for you, in
  an instant and truly, when
  the hard times come.

My girlfriends bless my life. Once
we were young, with no idea of the
incredible joys or the incredible sorrows that lay
ahead. Nor did we know how much we would need
each other.

Now I tell all young women to take my sister-in-law's
advice. Get yourself some girlfriends. You're gonna
need them.

— Author Unknown

Girlfriends Are Forever

The silver friend knows your present and the gold friend knows all of your past dirt and glories. Once in a blue moon there's someone who knows it all, someone who knows and accepts you unconditionally, someone who's there for life.

— Jill McCorkle

Nearly everything in this world
changes with time. Boyfriends
come and go. Kids grow up
and go out on their own. Jobs
change, home addresses change,
and even the best of marriages
can change over time. But your
girlfriends are forever.

— Carol Thomas

We Will Be Friends
for Life...

When we are old women
we will sit on the porch
and watch the leaves tremble
in autumn's breath
We will rock on rocking chairs
the lull of aged wood
creaking under our feet
We will wear pretty dresses
with purple flowers in our hair
and hum songs in our heads
to the beat of children's laughter
in the distance

We will say nothing at times
and that silence will be
our greatest solace
and other times we will talk for hours
or until the sun sinks into night
and the moon comes out to play
We will remember then
the days when life was defined
by complexity
when we danced in the moonlight
until the sun came out
and when we vowed our friendship
would last a lifetime

— Deana Marino

Ten Reasons Why We Are So Alike

Because we delight in
other women's "Bad Hair Days,"
and we blame how we look in swimsuits
on the dressing room lights;
Because we take more snack breaks
than we should
and only regret it a little;
Because we lose track of time
in fabric stores, bookstores,
and stores with cute clerks,
and there is always one more horrific dress
we can talk each other into trying on;
Because our kitchen table talks
have only changed in subject and drink,
and we probably keep the phone company
from going broke;
Because we both agree that men
should not be the ones designing bras
and that no actually doable
exercise video exists;
Because we are more than just
two women:
we are friends.

— Heidi Lebauer

A Poem
for My Girlfriend

When we are too old to wear miniskirts,
we will probably wear them anyway —
on days when we feel like it...
And when we are tired
of fighting the fight to prove
all women are equal,
all women are beautiful and strong,
to those who do not
understand us yet,
we will keep on fighting
with truth, knowledge, and love.
And when we have laughed
and cried more than our share,
more than "normal" people seem to, anyway,
still we will walk on.
And we will just keep going.
You are my sister, always.
You are a true heart, a fighter,
thinker, and dreamer.
You are sunshine.
You are a friend.

— Ashley Rice

A Girlfriend Is
the Greatest Friend
You Can Have

A girlfriend is someone who doesn't act
judgmental when you order dessert —
even if you're supposed to be on a diet.

A girlfriend is someone who tells you
when you have something in your teeth
or your zipper is down.

A girlfriend is someone who knows your
phone number by heart and can dial it
in 1.2 seconds flat.

A girlfriend is someone who treats for
coffee and doesn't keep watch of when
you're going to pay back the favor.

A girlfriend is someone who borrows your clothes... and actually returns them.

A girlfriend is someone who is always there with whatever remedy the situation requires — a shoulder to lean on, a hand to hold, or an inappropriate joke to get you smiling again.

A girlfriend is someone wonderful, loving, supportive, honest, accepting, reliable, understanding, and all-around amazing.

A girlfriend is one of the greatest friends you can have.

— Rachyl Taylor

Everything I Need to Know in Life I Learned from My Girlfriends

+ Good times are even better when they're shared.

+ A long talk can cure almost anything.

+ Everyone needs someone to share their secrets with.

+ Listening is just as important as talking.

+ An understanding friend is better than a therapist... and cheaper, too!

+ Laughter makes the world a happier place.

+ Friends are like wine; they get better with age.

+ Calories don't count when you are having lunch (or any other food) with your girlfriends.

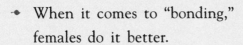

- Sometimes you just need a shoulder to cry on.

- Great minds think alike, especially when they are female!

- When it comes to "bonding," females do it better.

- You are never too old for a slumber party!

- Girls just want to have fun.

- It's important to make time to do "girl things."

- You can never have too many shoes.

- Gems may be precious, but friendship is priceless!

— Author Unknown

All I Need Is a Little Help from My Girlfriends

What do we live for, if it is
not to make life less difficult
for each other?

— George Eliot

To help one another is part of the religion of
our sisterhood.

— Louisa May Alcott

It is not so much our friends' help that helps us
as the confident knowledge that they will help us.

— Epicurus

Girlfriends Just Know

I know that if I need to vent, you are there to listen. And you know that if you need to borrow clothes, my closet's always open.

I know that if I ever need you, I can call — any hour, any day. And you know that if life gets crummy, you can lean on me for as long as you need.

I know that if my car was broken, you would give me a ride. And you know that if you fell on your knees, I would be there to pick you up.

I know that if it was raining really hard, you would share your umbrella with me. And you know that if you were feeling sick, I would visit and bring you flowers.

I know that no matter where I go, I will take our memories with me. And you know that as long as life goes on, we will always be friends.

— Elle Mastro

A Girlfriend's
Bill of Rights

1. A girlfriend has the right to borrow money, clothes, junk food, or any combination thereof, at any time, provided that such borrowing has been approved in advance.

2. In any given crisis situation (e.g., lost keys, lost purse, lost boyfriend), a girlfriend has the right to call at any time, including 2 A.M., no matter how trivial the crisis may seem the next day.

3. A girlfriend has the right to convey top secret information without risk of information being disclosed to other friends, boyfriends, or anyone else of importance.

4. In the event that one girlfriend
   is trying on jeans at a store, the
   observing friend has the right
   to indicate when such jeans are
   not flattering. In the event that
   jeans have already been purchased
   and taken home from store, the
   observing friend has the right,
   and duty, to insist that
   said jeans look fabulous
   no matter what.

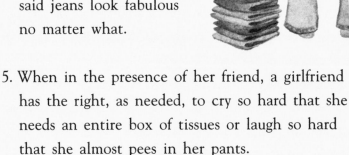

5. When in the presence of her friend, a girlfriend
   has the right, as needed, to cry so hard that she
   needs an entire box of tissues or laugh so hard
   that she almost pees in her pants.

6. A girlfriend has the right, at any time, to hug her
   friend for any reason... or for no reason at all.

— Melissa Simpson

It's a Girl Thing

I feel there is something unexplored about women that only a woman can explore.

— Georgia O'Keeffe

I have come to understand why girlfriends are so important. A husband — or any man, I suppose — may be an extraordinary human being and a best friend, but it is a very unusual man who can match some of the high standards of a really close girlfriend! I ask you... With whom but a girlfriend can you

...be shamelessly silly?

...reason in a totally illogical manner, without fear of judgment?

...blubber with guaranteed consolation?

...change your mind without explanation?

...recite endless details with no point?

...be absolutely honest about how much you spent for your clothes?

...review your husband's annoying habits with laughter?

...or rely on unqualified sympathy for an overweight body, an overdue period, or an overbearing mother-in-law?

— Joy MacKenzie

*O*nly another woman understands what it's like to be a woman. Only another woman knows just what you're feeling when you complain of cramps or PMS. Only another woman can appreciate the red shirt you found on the sale rack that goes just *perfectly* with your favorite black pants. Only another woman understands how important it is to find exactly the right picture for that wall, hung at exactly the right height, under exactly the right lighting. Scientists haven't acknowledged it yet, but the truth is that there's an infinite amount of knowledge and understanding bundled up in that extra X chromosome.

— Rachyl Taylor

*W*hether we are black or white, fat or thin, outgoing or shy, rich or poor, old or young, we are first and foremost female. Our common bond of feminine experience is stronger than any differences. There is something so essential and primordial in women sharing with other women. It seems the most natural thing in the world.

— BJ Gallagher

Top Ten Things
Only Women Understand

10. Why it's good to have five pairs of black shoes.

9. The difference between cream, ivory, and off-white.

8. Crying can be fun.

7. Fat clothes.

6. A salad, diet drink, and a hot fudge sundae make a balanced lunch.

5. Why discovering a designer dress on the clearance rack can be considered a peak life experience.

4. A good man might be hard to find, but a good hairdresser is next to impossible.

3. The inaccuracy of every bathroom scale ever made.

2. Why a phone call between two women never lasts under ten minutes.

AND THE NUMBER ONE THING ONLY WOMEN UNDERSTAND:

1. OTHER WOMEN!

— Author Unknown

Girlfriends Talk About Boyfriends...

𝓘t's no secret that women love to talk. We talk about people, places, clothes, movies, and food. We talk about our most intimate secrets: our dreams and worries, hopes and fears. We talk about work, home, life, love, kids, and stress. We laugh. We cry. And whenever we're laughing or crying the hardest, you can bet we're talking about just one thing: men.

— Rachyl Taylor

𝓞ne of the greatest things about girlfriends is having someone to talk with about men. When we're with our girlfriends, we can laugh about all those little quirks of his that usually drive us crazy. We can collaborate on how to deal with problems. And best of all, we can share secrets, tips, and advice to help each other understand what in the world those guys are all about.

— Carol Thomas

Girlfriend's Guy-Translation Dictionary

"CAN I HELP WITH DINNER?"
Translated: "Why isn't it already on the table?"

"UH-HUH," "SURE, HONEY," OR "YES, DEAR."
Translated: Absolutely nothing. It's a conditioned response.

"IT WOULD TAKE TOO LONG TO EXPLAIN."
Translated: "I have no idea how it works."

"TAKE A BREAK, HONEY, YOU'RE WORKING TOO HARD."
Translated: "I can't hear the game over the vacuum cleaner."

"THAT'S INTERESTING, DEAR."
Translated: "Are you still talking?"

"I CAN'T FIND IT."
Translated: "It didn't fall into my outstretched hands, so I'm completely clueless."

"WHAT DID I DO THIS TIME?"
Translated: "What did you catch me at?"

"YOU KNOW I COULD NEVER LOVE ANYONE ELSE."
Translated: "I am used to the way you yell at me and realize it could be worse."

"YOU LOOK TERRIFIC."
Translated: "I'm begging you, please, don't try on one more outfit, I'm starving."

— Becky Freeman

The Laughter of Friends...

Whoever said laughter is the best medicine was right — it's also the glue that holds friendships together. To laugh together at life's ridiculous turn of events makes those events bearable. To laugh at the funny things in life makes life wonderful. The real gift is having a friend to share... laughter with.

— Ellen Jacob

There's something different about the way two women laugh together: the kind of contagious laughter that starts over nothing and won't stop for anything — not for librarians or prayer time or irritated movie theater audiences. It's the kind that makes your cheeks ache and tears run down your face; the kind that makes you feel so good inside that it hurts; the kind that makes you feel alive and loved, happier to be wherever you are than you could possibly be anywhere else.

— Rachyl Taylor

One can never speak enough of the virtues, the dangers, the power of shared laughter.

— Françoise Sagan

Among those whom I like or admire, I can find no common denominator, but among those whom I love, I can: all of them make me laugh.

— W. H. Auden

Being crazy together can pull us through the tough times. So enjoy the laughs, and give humor the honor it deserves. If we can keep each other laughing, we can keep each other sane.

— Carmen Renee Berry and Tamara Traeder

Girl Talk...

*T*alk between women friends is always therapy.

— Jayne Anne Phillips

*T*alk is at the very heart of women's friendships, the core of the way women connect. It's the given, the absolute assumption of friendship.... In the flow of conversation, back and forth, women hear each other out, take each other seriously, care and feel cared for. When a friend calls with a serious problem while you're cooking dinner, the pot goes on the back burner. When something happens at work or home that you can't quite, exactly, figure out, you take all that raw undigested feeling to a safe place — a friend — and come away clearer.

— Ellen Goodman and Patricia O'Brien

We go straight to the gut.
It's more than girl talk;
it's soul talk.

— Laurin Sydney

Intimacies between women often go backwards,
beginning in revelations and ending in small talk.

— Elizabeth Bowen

Few comforts are more alluring for a woman than the
rich, intimate territory of women's talk. A woman friend
will say, "You are not alone. I have felt that way, too.
This is what happened to me." Home, in other words.

— Elsa Walsh

More than Words...

There is no need for an outpouring
of words to explain oneself to a friend
Friends understand each other's thoughts
even before they are spoken

— Susan Polis Schutz

A friend is someone you can be alone with and have
nothing to do and not be able to think of anything to
say and be comfortable in the silence.

— Sheryl Condie

The language of friendship is not words
but meanings.

— Henry David Thoreau

Friendship needs no studied phrases,
Polished face, or winning wiles;
Friendship deals no lavish praises,
Friendship dons no surface smiles.

Friendship follows Nature's diction,
Shuns the blandishments of art,
Boldly severs truth from fiction,
Speaks the language of the heart.

— Anonymous

Oh, for the love of a friend... one who lingers near my door in times of distress, and stretches out a hand... and who says little but feels largely; one whose very glance radiates tenderness, sympathy, and loving kindness... and who penetrates the very soul of me.

— Mae Lawson

Getting Real...

The best thing about girlfriends is that we can be whoever we are with them, and they will accept us anyway. No persona required, we can be cranky or perky — and both may be annoying — with greasy hair and a sweater two sizes too small that's covered with ugly little balls. It really does not matter to our close friends what we look like or what mood we're in.

— Carmen Renee Berry and Tamara Traeder

If you have just one person with whom you can be weak, miserable and contrite, and who won't hurt you for it, then you are rich.

— Margarete Buber-Neumann

Oh, the comfort, the inexpressible comfort of feeling safe with a person; having neither to weigh thoughts nor measure words, but to pour them all out, just as they are, chaff and grain together, knowing that a faithful hand will take and sift them, keep what is worth keeping, and then, with the breath of kindness, blow the rest away.

— George Eliot

Accepting one another without reservation is part of the magic about friendship. When behavior that ought to drive you crazy makes you laugh instead, then you know you've found a true friend.

— Ellen Jacob

Circle of Friends

The soul selects her own society.

— Emily Dickinson

*W*omen have the luxury of creating their very own support network, tailor-made to fit all their needs. Every friend fills a different role. There are friends who are perfect for going out with and friends who are perfect for staying home with; friends who are great at keeping secrets and friends who will dish out all the latest gossip; friends who will support you on your new diet and friends who will help you cheat on it. Having a well-chosen circle of friends is like having your own private round table. They are your support system, your lifeline to the world.

— Natalie Evans

A Woman Can Never Have Too Many...

pairs of shoes,

books on her nightstand,

little black dresses,

candles in her home,

favorite songs,

tubes of lipstick,

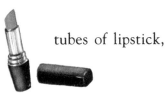

inside jokes with her friends,

photos on the wall,

dreams for her future,
memories of her past...

or *girlfriends!*

— Amy Hinz Horn

The 5 Friends
Every Woman Needs

The "I've seen you with braces and bell-bottoms" friend
This is the one that knows where you live. Not only literally, but that figurative place where it all began. You bonded over jumping rope, passing notes, and gushing over teen idols. She knows your family, how you crashed your first car into a pole the day after your sixteenth birthday, and she didn't laugh when you wore a 32 AAA bra. Your friendship is based on the deep roots that come from knowing each other through all the big and little events that propel us into adulthood. She understands where you are coming from and helps you get where you want to go.

The biological buddy
This is the friend that mirrors your family status. If you have children, so does she, and hopefully her kids are close enough in age to yours that you can bemoan the dilemmas of potty training or car seats together. You listen patiently to her stories about junior, nod in the right places and then it's your turn. You swoop in in a crunch to babysit or pick the kids up from school and vice versa. It's a beautiful thing. On the flipside, this friend may be the one among your group that, like you, doesn't have children. Together you celebrate your freewheeling status at fancy restaurants where you couldn't find a high chair to save your life. You go to museum openings, see movies with subtitles, and indulge in marathon shopping excursions. Don't call me before 9 A.M.? No worries about getting any guff, she too is still asleep.

Your own personal domestic diva

She knows everything from how to get candle wax off your cat's ear to what color shoes to wear with a celadon silk suit. Need a recipe for champagne punch? She'll fax over five of them and would make the champagne if she needed to. Roof leaking? She's there with some shingles and tar that she happened to have in the workshop. She has every tool, every recipe, and every magazine article cross-referenced and indexed, and she's as resourceful as the FBI, CIA, and Interpol combined. She is irreplaceable.

Your sister-in-a-suit

She knows how much your salary is and was instrumental in getting it there by counseling you before your last big performance review. You share investment tips, career strategies, and the secrets of crafting the world's perfect resume. What to wear to that interview? She's the one you turn to. Powerhouse, confidante, and the *Wall Street Journal* in comfortable pumps — she's a source of professional inspiration and awfully fun to have drinks with after work, to boot.

Wild woman

Nothing will shock her, and the word judgment (for better or worse) is not in her vocabulary. You can tell her anything. No matter how serious or benign, she takes it in stride on her way to the next adventure. When you're with her, hang on tight and never use your real name.

— Ame Mahler Beanland and Emily Miles Terry

Sisterly Support

$\mathcal{I}$ often think, how could I have survived without these women?

— Claudette Renner

$\mathcal{S}$ome people we can always depend upon for making the best, instead of the worst, of whatever happens. For all of us have some friends, or friend, to whom we instinctively carry every one of our griefs or vexations, assured that if anyone can help us, they can and will.

— Anonymous

$\mathcal{S}$ometimes it is a slender thread,
Sometimes a strong, stout rope;
She clings to one end,
I the other;
She calls it friendship;
I call it hope.

— Lois Wyse

Your boss is mad; your spouse is complaining; the kids are cranky; and you just discovered that the roof is leaking. There's only one thing to do. Pick up the phone and call a friend.

After all, who but a good friend would put her life on hold in order to listen, advise, sympathize, and send you on your way secure in the knowledge that someone cares?

A good friend is a connection to life — a tie to the past, a road to the future, the key to sanity in a totally insane world....

When we bare our souls and tell the stories of bad bosses, sagging roofs, crying kids, and moping mates, we are really asking others to share our lives and our love. For even as we tell our stories of life gone wrong, we know we are on the way to patching our quilts.

We know because our friends listen, advise, and then promise us everything will come out just fine.

Most of all, we know in our hearts that good things will happen because we have friends willing to light the dark passages and rejoice with us at the end of the long, hard journey.

In sunshine and in sorrow, we look for those who will always stand with us.

And we know all that really matters is that we are not alone so long as we can call one person *friend*.

— Lois Wyse

Simple vs. Real Friends

A simple friend has never seen you cry.
A real friend has shoulders soggy from your tears.

A simple friend doesn't know your parents'
first names.
A real friend has their phone numbers in
her address book.

A simple friend brings a bottle of wine to your party.
A real friend comes early to help you cook and stays late
to help you clean.

A simple friend hates it when you call after she has gone
to bed.
A real friend asks why you took so long to call.

A simple friend seeks to talk with you about your problems.
A real friend seeks to help you with your problems.

A simple friend wonders about your romantic history.
A real friend could blackmail you with it.

A simple friend, when visiting, acts like a guest.
A real friend opens your refrigerator and helps herself.

A simple friend thinks the friendship is over when you
    have an argument.
A real friend knows that it's not a friendship until after
    you've had a fight.

A simple friend expects you to always be there for her.
A real friend expects to always be there for you!

— Author Unknown

18 Ways to Let
Your Girlfriend Know
You Care About Her...

1. Think of her often. And smile.

2. Find time to spend together, because that time will always be well spent.

3. Laugh together. Often!

4. Don't be afraid to talk about big things... or little ones.

5. Think of her first when you have something exciting to share.

6. Don't sing (unless it's her birthday).

7. Feel totally comfortable in your relationship, yet respect its boundaries.

8. Let nothing ever come between the two of you, except an occasional ice-cream sundae (with extra sprinkles).

9. Share clothes.

10. Share heartaches as well as joys.

11. Share secrets, but only with each other.

12. Don't ever be afraid to act silly together.

13. Talk, talk, talk.

14. Be comfortable in the silence.

15. Don't judge.

16. Remember: One hug is worth a thousand phone calls.

17. Be an awesome listener.

And the most important way to let your girlfriend know you care about her...

18. Tell her so!

— Donna Gephart

A Thank-You
to My Girlfriend

Thank you for all the warmth.
The listening that goes deeper
than hearing my spoken words.
Thank you for gentle advice and for
sharing smile-making remedies that
can cure any case of the blues.

For truly, absolutely inspiring me.
For giving me enough leeway to
be a little crazy without ever
holding it against me.
For letting me know that the bridge
that exists between us will rise
above whatever comes along.

— Ann Turrell

You're a Great Friend...

You're there to lean on when I'm hurt,
to laugh with (we do a lot of that),
to give me that little kick
when I need a boost,
and to offer me direction
when my life gets a little out of focus.
What would I do without our
endless phone conversations
or our "ladies' nights out"?
We always have a good time;
you add something to my life
that was never really there before.
You're the best, and for that
and everything else...
thanks.

— Julia Escobar

Girls Just Want to Have FUN

Making Time for the Girls

With all of life's responsibilities and distractions, sometimes it can be hard to find time for fun. When you've got one too many items on your to-do list, it's easy to put off spending time with your girlfriends, telling yourself you'll call "next week" or that you'll get together "next month." But that's a big mistake. It's when things are busiest and most chaotic that you need time with your girlfriends more than ever.

Time with the girls is like therapy, giving you a chance to put everything else aside and just be you. When you're with your girlfriends, it doesn't matter if your shirt has a stain on it, if you're having a bad hair day, or if you haven't shaved your legs in months. All that matters is that you're there, taking time off from the rest of the world, and sharing some memorable moments with the women who mean the most to you.

So whether you decide to hit the clubs for a ladies' night out or meet at someone's house for a movie marathon, just remember that the time you spend with your girlfriends is always time well spent. Keep reading for some ideas that will hopefully give you a little inspiration to pick up the phone and get together with your girlfriends!

Make a Date...

Whoever came up with the idea that dating is just for love relationships was crazy. The best way to keep your girlfriends at the top of your priority list (where they belong) is by making dates with them. Set a time and a place to get together, and enforce a "no flaking out" policy.

If you've got a few girlfriends who live a little farther away, don't let distance stand between you. Set a phone date for a time when you're both available to curl up on the couch for a few hours and catch up on all the latest.

It's a Date!
3 Fun Outings for Girlfriends

Spa Day: You've always dreamed of getting away to one of those spas for a day of massages, facials, pedicures, and all-around bliss. Stop waiting for a special occasion and go ahead and indulge. And who better to go with than your girlfriends?

Ladies' Night: Put on your sexiest attire, hit the clubs, and dance the night away. Remember: no boys allowed! Make a game of it by seeing who can come up with the most original way to ward off a guy's unwanted advances, then let the winner pick the next ladies' night destination.

Mid-Week Lunch: What could be better than escaping the office on Tuesday or Wednesday and taking a three-hour lunch with a girlfriend? Don't forget to discuss work for a sentence or two so that you can write it off as a business expense!

Go Shopping...

There is no denying the fact that women love to shop. But there is one thing that women love to do even more than go shopping: go shopping with their girlfriends. When you see women at the mall, they aren't just shopping. They are spending something much more important than money; they are spending *time*. Those hours spent walking from store to store are valuable hours spent talking, bonding, and sharing.

So go ahead, grab a girlfriend and hit the mall. Forget about the outside world for an afternoon and indulge in a little shop therapy. Whatever damage it does to your wallet is worth the good it will do for your friendship!

Top 5 Reasons It's Better to Shop with Women

- There's no need to waste any time in stores that sell computers, hardware, or anything that can be referred to as a "gadget."

- She knows how important it is to pick out *just the right* drapes and *just the right* finials. (And she knows what a finial is.)

- When she tells you something looks good on you, it's because it looks good on you, not because she's ready to leave.

- If you find a fabulous dress, she tells you to buy it and doesn't ask when or where you'll wear it.

- She understands how you can spend an entire day at the mall, spend $200, and come home with one tiny bag.

Plan a Girls' Getaway...

Coordinate a girlfriend retreat. Rent a cabin, go hiking...
explore a foreign country, or send your kids to Grandma's
and take turns hosting at your own homes. The destination
is only the beginning of the journey. Coordinating
something like this is tough, so be prepared for lots of back
and forth, but once you reach consensus on a date and
place, stick to it and try to make it an annual event. We
know ladies who pay "dues" at their monthly girls' nights
and use the money for an annual weekend retreat. If you're
spread out around the country, you can individually
maintain Buddy Banks and save money for the plane
tickets and expenses of converging in one place. Think of
all the trouble you can get into. Make a pact: What
happens on retreat, stays on retreat!

— Ame Mahler Beanland and Emily Miles Terry

Girls' Getaway Rules

- Have as much fun as possible.
- Make at least one juicy confession.
- Keep all secrets.
- Do NOT, under any circumstances, get eight hours of sleep.
- If you can't sing well, sing loud.
- No dieting while on vacation.
- No men allowed.
- Break all rules that interfere with girls' getaway rules.

Traveling with a friend can be glorious... Nothing is so rewarding as successfully following directions in another language (which neither of you speak very well, or at all) or viewing the Grand Canyon together for the first time or finding a restaurant that's not in a guidebook, complete with delicious local fare and an absence of other tourists. Nothing can bond you with your friend like escaping a scary-looking man who seems to be following you or the hilarity of watching American men gawk at topless women on a French beach....

Traveling with a friend implies that you will become roommates, at least temporarily.... You will learn more things about her and about your relationship than you ever thought possible. Some of these things will be niggling and annoying; random thoughts of ditching her in a gas station may come up. More than likely, however, you will become better friends for having lived through it; you will know each other better, have a greater abundance of embarrassing recollections with which to tease each other, and generally have stored away a unique basket of memories.

— Carmen Renee Berry and Tamara Traeder

Catch a Movie...

Do you need a break from the days of your life but don't have time for a real vacation? Take a day off, call up a girlfriend and ask her to go with you to celebrate your freedom with a movie and lunch out. Are you carrying around pent-up emotions and want to cry, but can't seem to get started? Rent a surefire tearjerker video and have a bunch of girlfriends over for a rip-roarin' Sap Fest. Because the stereotypical chick flick isn't just something to laugh at. It is a wonderful something to cry at, too. Just don't forget the popcorn and plenty of tissues.

— Becky Freeman

Classic Chick Flicks

A League of Their Own

Beaches

Boys on the Side

Clueless

Emma

Fried Green Tomatoes

Girls Just Wanna Have Fun

Mystic Pizza

Shag

Sixteen Candles

Steel Magnolias

The Joy Luck Club

The Truth About Cats and Dogs

Thelma and Louise

Waiting to Exhale

Start a Book Club...

Get a group of your best girlfriends together once a month for a book club meeting. Reading the same books will give you a chance to bond and share your thoughts on topics that you might not usually discuss. Not only will you get to enjoy each other's company, you'll learn a lot about each other's tastes, interests, and opinions. You might be surprised at what you'll find out about your girlfriends!

Classic Chick Books

Bridget Jones's Diary

Circle of Friends

Little Women

Midwives

One True Thing

Sense and Sensibility

She's Come Undone

Summer Sisters

The Divine Secrets of the Ya-Ya Sisterhood

The Hours

The Poisonwood Bible

The Red Tent

The Women of Brewster Place

Where the Heart Is

White Oleander

Have a Beauty Night...

There's something wonderfully indulgent and — let's face it — fabulously prissy about a bunch of friends fellowshipping in the name of toenail painting, facial masking, and manicuring. Perhaps it's the old-fashioned power of connecting with your inner glamour-puss or simply the sheer chickcentricity of giggling over a foofy libation. No matter your beauty style, a night of feminine indulgence is a powerful bonding ritual. Who can be self-conscious or aloof while sporting a mask of green gooey mud?...

Beauty Night!
Place: Amanda's house
Date: Sat. March 18th
Time: 8 o'clock
Bring: one beauty secret

Send out an invitation and elect each person to bring an item or share a secret beauty potion. Or you can support a local gal's mission to drive that pink Cadillac by calling on a Mary Kay consultant or other trained professional. Be sure to have lots of clean towels on hand, plastic tubs for foot soaking, cotton balls, cotton swabs, and beauty basics like nail polish remover, headbands, and moisturizer.

Don't forget the food and drink. Go spa-inspired with pitchers of spring water with floating cucumber slices and fruit or make white wine spritzers. For food, think bite-sized snacks such as sliced fruits, crackers, and dips. Set a relaxed mood with candles, music, and lots of comfy pillows for reclining and lolling about. Pop *Steel Magnolias* in the VCR and pretend you're all at Truvy's.

...or a Beast Night

We've all had moments when we would rather shave our heads than take the time to carefully coif and blow-dry our hair, and the idea of beauty parlor night when you feel like a troll might be tough to swallow. So, as an alternative to beautification, how about beastification? Here is a formula for a debaucherous, all-you-can-eat, late night chickfest:

Your Garb: All the clothes your mother hates to see you in — your ratty jeans, stained sweats, and old shoes.

Makeup: None, or just enough so the fire department won't think you're a corpse if they show up.

The Crowd: All your best gals (leaving out the ones who never have a bad hair day or those who never pig out).

The Decor: Your apartment strewn with pillows and plenty of spots to dump food and drinks.

The Pig Out: Think salt and sugar — Velveeta® salsa cheese dip with tortilla chips, brie, salsa, chocolate dipping sauce and plenty of strawberries, s'mores (melt the marshmallows in the microwave and use the chocolate dipping sauce), chocolate chip cookie dough, and ice cream!

The Libations: Soda, wine, beer, and martinis.

The Festivities: Paint your toenails black, crank call all your ex-boyfriends, and watch *Thelma and Louise*.

The Gab: Everything from guys to politics to body hair and career advancement.

Soundtrack: Pat Benatar, The Dixie Chicks, Sister Sledge, Gloria Gaynor, Carole King, Indigo Girls.

— Ame Mahler Beanland and Emily Miles Terry

Start a Supper Club...

For centuries, women everywhere have bonded over food. Whether talking in the kitchen while preparing a meal or sitting and chatting over lunch, there is something about the ritual of preparing and eating food that inspires women to pour their hearts out to each other.

One way you can take advantage of this is by starting a supper club. Pick a group of your favorite (and most culinary-adept) girlfriends and get together once a month to share some food, recipes, and laughter. You can make the preparation part of the fun by doing the cooking together, or you can each prepare a portion of the meal and meet at someone's house to do the eating. Not only will you have a chance to spend valuable time with your girlfriends, you're sure to build up your recipe collection as well!

Of course, we all know that no gathering of women would be complete without chocolate. Here's a recipe for a five-star dessert that's sure to get rave reviews from your girlfriends...

Double-Chocolate Peanut Butter Brownies

3 ounces bittersweet chocolate
1 ounce unsweetened chocolate
¾ stick unsalted butter, cut into pieces
¾ cup sugar
1 teaspoon vanilla
2 large eggs
½ teaspoon salt
½ cup all-purpose flour
½ cup peanut butter morsels

1. Preheat oven to 350°F. Lightly butter and flour an 8-inch square baking pan.

2. Melt chocolates and butter in a large, heavy saucepan over low heat, stirring until smooth. Remove from heat. Whisk in sugar and vanilla. Whisk in eggs, one at a time, until smooth and glossy. Stir in salt and flour until just combined. Stir in peanut butter morsels.

3. Spread batter evenly in prepared pan and bake on middle rack of oven for 25 to 30 minutes, or until toothpick comes out with small crumbs sticking to it. Cool brownies completely on baking rack. Cut into 16 squares.

Make a Pact...

Remember when you were a kid, how you and your
blood sister made a solemn oath to be friends till the
end of time? Just because you're all grown up doesn't
mean you can't still promise to be friends forever.
Maybe you can do without the actual blood this time
around, but go ahead and put your feelings into words
to let a special girlfriend know how much she means
to you... and how much she always will.

I promise that nothing will ever change the amount
of appreciation I have for you. I promise that if I ever
have news to share, you'll always be first on the call list.
I promise — if I ever release a genie from a magic lamp —
I'll share my three wishes with you. In the event that
never happens, I promise that you're welcome to split
any pizza I might have in my possession. (And the
same goes for chocolate.)

I promise I will be there to see you through anything
that tries to get you down. I promise that I'll be around
through it all; I'll support you in your efforts; I'll believe
in you at all times; we'll do whatever it takes and together
we'll chase away the clouds and keep the sun shining in
our lives.

— Jean Roberts

One of the most special
places in my heart will always be
       saved for you.
You...
    the one person I can always talk to;
    the one person who understands.
You...
    for making me laugh in the rain;
    for helping me shoulder my troubles.
You...
    for loving me in spite of myself,
    and always putting me
       back on my feet again.
You...
    for giving me someone to believe in;
    someone who lets me know that
    there really is goodness

      and kindness
       and laughter and love
        in the world.
You...
    for being one of the best
    parts of my life, and proving it
      over and over again.

— Robin Hardt

ACKNOWLEDGMENTS

We gratefully acknowledge the permission granted by the following authors, publishers, and authors' representatives to reprint poems or excerpts from their publications.

Andrews McMeel Publishing for "Laugh and the world..." by Laurie Kuslansky and "A friend is someone you can..." by Sheryl Condie from WITTY WORDS FROM WISE WOMEN, edited by BJ Gallagher Hateley. Copyright © 2002 by BJ Gallagher Hateley. All rights reserved. And for "Whoever said laughter is the best medicine..." and "Accepting one another..." by Ellen Jacob and "We go straight..." by Laurin Sydney from YOU'RE THE BEST FRIEND EVER by Ellen Jacob. Copyright © 2001 by Ellen Jacob. All rights reserved.

Red Wheel/Weiser for "Where would I be..." and "Whether we are..." from EVERYTHING I NEED TO KNOW I LEARNED FROM OTHER WOMEN by BJ Gallagher. Copyright © 2002 by BJ Gallagher. All rights reserved. And for "The 5 Friends Every Woman Needs," "Coordinate a girlfriend retreat...," "There's something wonderfully indulgent...," and "We've all had moments when..." from IT'S A CHICK THING by Ame Mahler Beanland and Emily Miles Terry. Copyright © 2000 by Ame Mahler Beanland and Emily Miles Terry. All rights reserved.

Wildcat Canyon Press for "Being crazy together...," "The best thing about...," and "Traveling with a..." from GIRLFRIENDS: INVISIBLE BONDS, ENDURING TIES by Carmen Renee Berry and Tamara Traeder. Copyright © 1995 by Carmen Renee Berry and Tamara C. Traeder. All rights reserved.

Barbara Cage for "Girlfriends Are the Best Friends of All." Copyright © 2004 by Barbara Cage. All rights reserved.

Susan M. Catalano for "A Woman Needs a Friend...." Copyright © 2004 by Susan M. Catalano. All rights reserved.

Harvest House Publishers, Eugene, OR 97402, for "I imagine we are all...," "Girlfriend's Guy-Translation Dictionary," and "Do you need..." from COFFEE CUP FRIENDSHIPS & CHEESECAKE FUN by Becky Freeman. Copyright © 2001 by Becky Freeman. All rights reserved. Used by permission.

Jill McCorkle for "The silver friend..." from "Cathy, Now and Then." Copyright © 1996 by Jill McCorkle. All rights reserved.

Heidi Lebauer for "Ten Reasons Why We Are So Alike." Copyright © 2004 by Heidi Lebauer. All rights reserved.

Georgia O'Keeffe for "I feel there is something unexplored...." Copyright © by Georgia O'Keeffe. All rights reserved.

Zondrevan for "I have come to understand why..." from FRIENDS THROUGH THICK AND THIN by Sue Buchanan, Joy MacKenzie, Gloria L. Gaither, and Peggy Benson. Copyright © 1998 by Gloria Gaither, Sue Buchanan, Peggy Benson, and Joy MacKenzie. All rights reserved.

Françoise Sagan for "One can never speak enough of...." Copyright © by Françoise Sagan. All rights reserved.

Random House, Inc., for "Among those whom I like..." by W. H. Auden from THE DYER'S HAND AND OTHER ESSAYS, edited by Edward Mendelson. Copyright © 1948, 1950, 1953, 1954, © 1956, 1957, 1958, 1960, 1962 by W. H. Auden. Copyright renewed 1975, 1977, 1980, 1982, 1984, 1985 by William Meredith and Monroe K. Spears. Copyright renewed 1988 by William Meredith. All rights reserved.

Jayne Anne Phillips for "Talk between women friends..." from "Road Trip: The Real Thing." Copyright © 1994 by Jayne Anne Phillips. All rights reserved.

Simon & Schuster Adult Publishing Group for "Talk is at the very heart..." from I KNOW JUST WHAT YOU MEAN by Ellen Goodman and Patricia O'Brien. Copyright © 2000 by Ellen Goodman and Patricia O'Brien. All rights reserved. And for "Few comforts are more alluring..." from DIVIDED LIVES: The Public and Private Lives of Three American Women by Elsa Walsh. Copyright © 1995 by Elsa Walsh. All rights reserved.

Elizabeth Bowen for "Intimacies between women...." Copyright © by Elizabeth Bowen. All rights reserved.

Margarete Buber-Neumann for "If you have just one person..." from Milena. Copyright © by Margarete Buber-Neumann. All rights reserved.

Amy Hinz Horn for "A Woman Can Never Have Too Many...." Copyright © 2004 by Amy Hinz Horn. All rights reserved.

Claudette Renner for "I often think, how could I...." Copyright © by Claudette Renner. All rights reserved.

William Morris Agency for "Sometimes it is a slender thread..." and "Your boss is mad..." from WOMEN MAKE THE BEST FRIENDS by Lois Wyse, published by Simon & Schuster, Inc. Copyright © 1995 by Lois Wyse. All rights reserved. Lois Wyse is the author or editor of numerous books, including: Funny, You Don't Look like a Grandmother; Kid You Sing My Songs; Company Manners; My Mother and Me; Kiss, Inc.; Grandchildren Are So Much Fun I Should Have Had Them First; and Nesting: Tales of Love, Life, and Real Estate.

Donna Gephart for "18 Ways to Let Your Girlfriend Know You Care About Her." Copyright © 2004 by Donna Gephart. All rights reserved.

Julia Escobar for "You're a Great Friend." Copyright © 2004 by Julia Escobar. All rights reserved.

Becky Milanski for "Double-Chocolate Peanut Butter Brownies." Copyright © 2004 by Becky Milanski. All rights reserved.

A careful effort has been made to trace the ownership of selections used in this anthology in order to obtain permission to reprint copyrighted material and give proper credit to the copyright owners. If any error or omission has occurred, it is completely inadvertent, and we would like to make corrections in future editions provided that written notification is made to the publisher:

BLUE MOUNTAIN ARTS, INC., P.O. Box 4549, Boulder, Colorado 80306.